The Night Is What It Eats

CODHILL
PRESS

Also by Danielle Hanson

Poetry Collections

Ambushing Water
(Brick Road Poetry Press)

Fraying Edge of Sky
(Codhill Press)

Anthology

Objects in This Mirror
co-edited with Julia Beach (Press 53)

The Night Is What It Eats

poems by

DANIELLE HANSON

―――――――

CODHILL PRESS

NEW YORK · NEW PALTZ

CODHILL
PRESS

codhill.com

Published in the United States of America
Library of Congress Control Number: 2025950780

ISBN 978-1-949933-35-2

Cover illustration by Coral Black
Author Photo by Kelley Klein
Cover and Book Design by Lorna Leighton
flytedesign.net

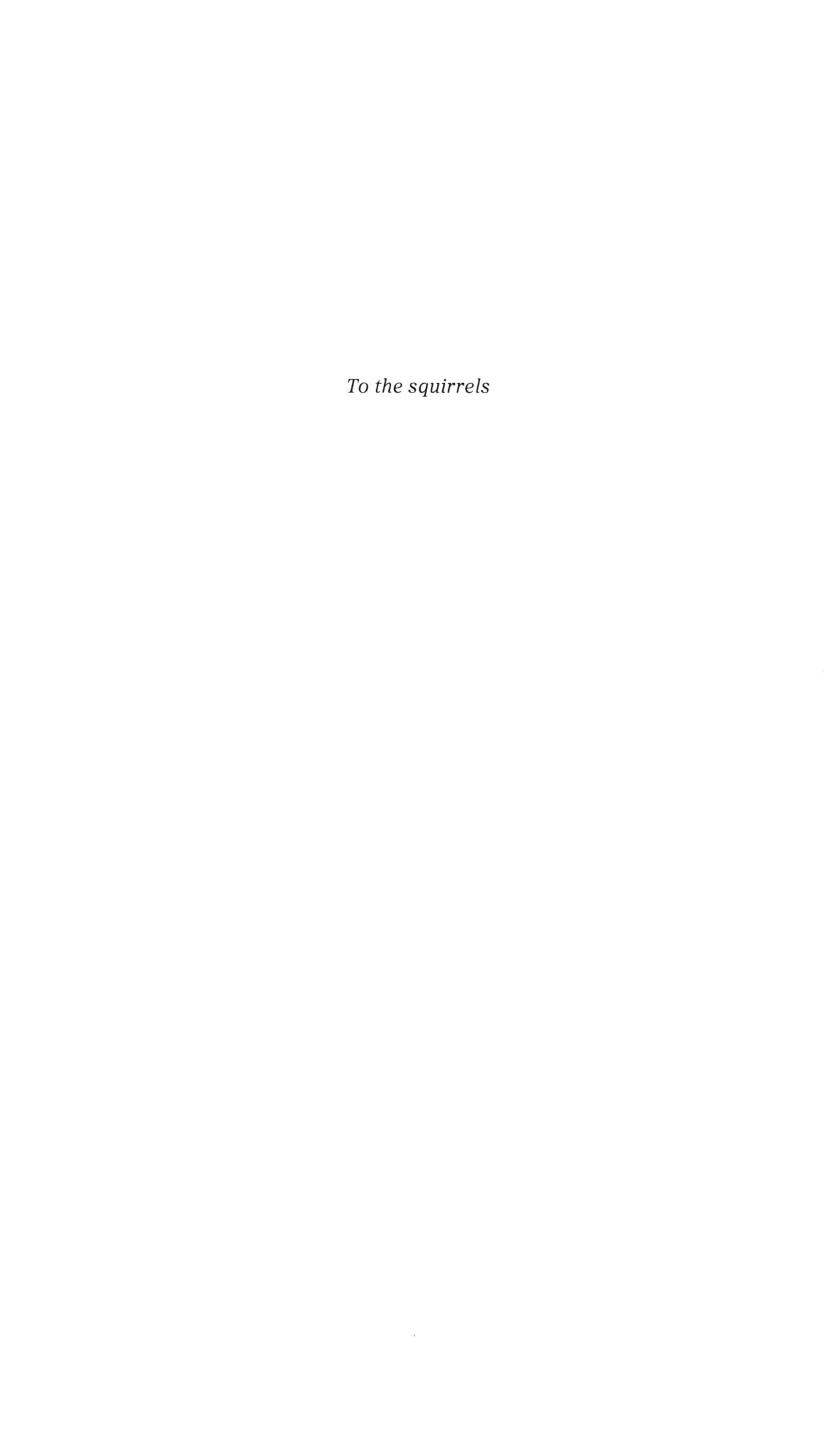

To the squirrels

CONTENTS

The Bird's Answer

A Dry River

A Journey Of Many Days

Asking For Tea

The Very Lip Of Her Lip

A Horrible Thing

The Bird's Answer

Aphorisms for the Eyes

An eye is a jellyfish caught from the see.

A glass eye is like a fake accent.

An eye is the most fragile thing you can't drop.

A goddess decorating a tree with eyes.

The eyes will always have it.

A tear is the fruit of the eye.

How does one look for a lost eye?

An eye is a target.

There are two eyes in I.

The lashes are the gates of the eyes.

Not only cloudy eyes produce rain.

He was sentenced to a thousand eyelashes.
    He asked for a thousand more.

St Lucia in the Afterlife

Hoping to give
my dowry to
the poor, I
rejected my suitor.
When he brought
police to kill me,
I gave him
my eyes he admired
so much. I try
to continue my acts
of charity here. I gave
Denis my head, peeled
off skin for Barnabas.
I try to give everyone
a hand. The items are
returned; the recipients
horrified. I won't give
up my vows. I
will hide my presents
under beds, among cloaks.
May the Lord bless us all
and keep all our parts.

Naming

Naming something is committing it to memory. Death,
hovering over a field, is called *Eurasian kestrel*.
Mountain invading sky is called *Alp*, or *Himalaya*, or . . .
The startling of day into hiding, like a doe in the forest,
is called *night*, and now *doe* and *forest* can take residence
in our brains. Day, peaking from the corner to see
if it's safe, is called *stars*, but never *moon*, never *flashlight*
    or *firefly*.
A rock has always been a rock, even a toddler knows,
and there's no sense in naming it.

Henhouse

The cloud is guarding the henhouse.
The babies disappear one by one
in the lick of fog–oh, Mother,
only the legs are left standing.
The blackberry bodies are
sky now–feet are
part of ground–the chickens
have become gods, sewing Heaven
to earth with their needles of beaks.
Oh, Mother, they are coming for us.

Hawk

A shriek brought us to the side
yard where a hawk stood eyeing
us—*regal* might be the word, *majestic.*
Both come from the Latin,
signify higher status, elevation.
The hawk is not an eagle.
They are of the same family
Accipitridae. Both
are birds of prey,
different from *pray.*
Both are angels of death.

The eagle is a symbol for the Gospel
of John which begins, *In the beginning*
was the Word, and the Word was
with God, and the Word was God.
John is the only Gospel not related
to the others, not *synoptic,*
which comes from the Greek *to eye.*

When we yelled, the hawk lifted
heavenward, and we could see
what was left in earth, our bantam,
the most beautiful of our flock and the most
skittish. It is understandable
how you can hate the hawk
despite its beauty.
It is wildness that attacks love,
untamed angel.

Sometimes the Angel of Death misses—
the beak not piercing the brain. Sometimes
all that is taken is an eye.

Daphne

She was already
unbound, long hair
flowing, legs growing
roots into the ground.
When she stretched
upwards, one could
hear wrens flutter
and settle, small
clicks and the crackle
of bones.

Fog and Birds

It's the fog that twitters in the mountains.
The sound solidifying out of air. As morning
progresses, the fog lightens little by little as
each sound flies off, as the hawk of sun descends,
talons out.
             Chickens scatter when they see a hawk,
then reform a flock when it passes. Little clouds
greeting each other. When I was a child, we lived
near the top of a mountain. On the steep sides
we made a fort of an abandoned coop. On foggy mornings
the world would stop being. We would become unbound.
Small birds would gather on the deck to eat the scattered
seeds. We would listen to their sounds. It felt that
time had paused and we would be forever.
It didn't even feel like we were being hunted by the sky.

Hawk

The hawk cannot help
but be a hungry angel.
The lake asks every day
what color it should be
and the sky always answers blue.
And you will be dust no matter
how many candles are lit for the dead.

What was it that took you
like a hawk plucks a bird
into a tree, berry of blood?
Eating disorder? Alcohol?
We hadn't spoken for years, since I held
a mirror to you in the hospital
and made you look.
What color was the sky
outside the hospital window?
Inside the hallway was an aviary
painted with too-blue sky.

I'd watch it for hours while you slept.
We had infants at home needing fed,
your blood to wash from our clothes,
so we took turns sitting with you.
You asked for a brush and a mirror
seemed unconcerned with our concern.
You'd been through it all before—
bulimia at fourteen, alcoholism at twenty—
but this was my first time so I studied,
made notes for you to take home.

For years you seemed to make it.
The surprise of your obituary:
found alone in your apartment.
It was morning, the sky was blue,
hovering.

Pecking Order

We're having trouble
reintroducing the wounded bantam
to the flock. She's a quarter-
sized chicken. The others have
brains too small to form intent.
They peck her head,
mimicking the hawk's
desire to reach soft brain.
She lays flat, showing her
willingness to submit.
Wings spread, head down,
earthing herself until well past
their anger. Take root,
smallness, become Daphne,
the tree not taken.

The Invention of the Feather Bed

As the hands of the farm wife closed
on the soft warm neck of the hen,
she dreamed of sleep
and the bird answered.

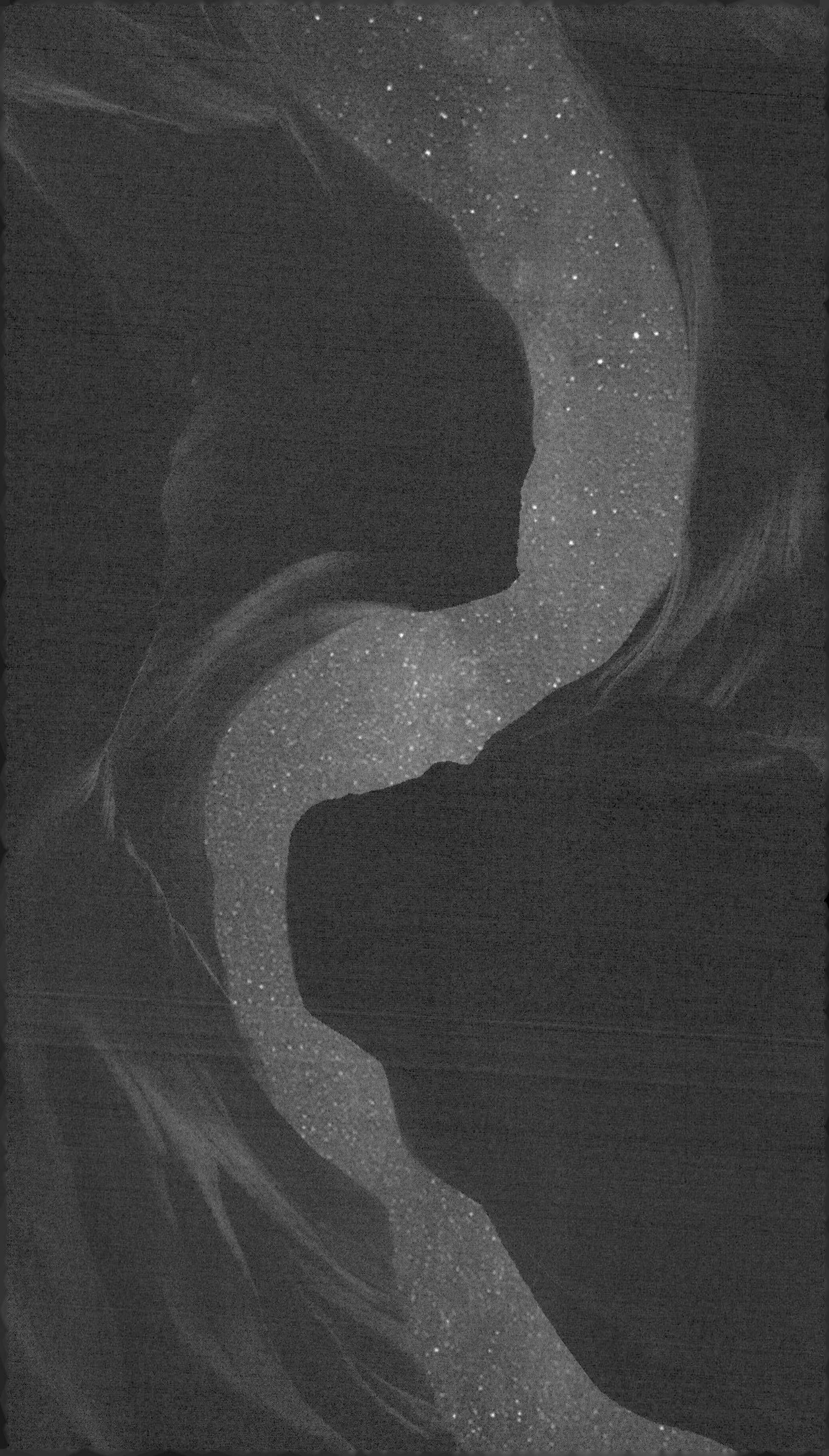

A
Dry
River

Aphorisms for the Hair

Hair is a dry river.

Hair gathers the wind in its mouth.

She made him wait while she dropped her hairs
    one by one to the floor.

Hair is always daring gravity.

Hair is a single organism desiring to cover the earth.

Hair licks the head.

Hair was the calling card she left in his drain.

If hair could sing we would all go deaf.

The hair crawled away at night to camp under the couch.

Hair is a nest for dreams.

The weight of her hair kept him from leaving.

A strand of hair hid so successfully it lost itself in sleep.

The flock of hair swarmed the head as night fell.

St Agnes in the Afterlife

I spend so much of my days
combing and braiding, I'm not sure
if I'm in Heaven or Purgatory.
The stream of pleas from teenage
drama queens is as endless as time.
They worry about backstabbing friends,
but when I was their age, I was dragged
through the streets naked and stabbed
through the throat. Try being popular
when your body has covered itself
in hair and any boy who liked you
(even if they were the worst)
has been blinded. My head
is on display in a case in Rome,
perpetually grounded, but please
go on about your inability to match
your eye shadow to your shirt. At least
I have my lamb to keep me company,
although I often lose her in the clouds,
or find her with the Virgin Mary,
who teases me with "Who
has a little lamb now?" Through all this,
my hair still grows. May it one day cover us all.

Fitting

Nature has a way of fitting
everything into its place
like a tightly-packed box.
Each grass of a field in succession—
telling us once is never
enough. A wild violet
next to a bed of pansies
calls human law into question.
Stream wearing down rocks
until they are no longer rocks—
relentless. There is always festering in stillness.
Harrier hawk killing sparrow
in an old cemetery, after circling
once, twice . . .

St Denis in the Afterlife

Had I known this head
would never shut up,
I would have left it
where it fell in the dirt.
Eternity is a long time
to hear *Repent* on repeat.
To think, I lugged this judgmental
stone up the highest
mountain to that refrain.
And as time (whatever
that means now)
trods on, the sermon
unravels, seeps and trickles:
Repent . . . Represent . . . Resent . . .
That last one is the truth.
Night after night, I dream of burying
this unwound brain into ground.
Every night, I dream vines grow
from the grave, leaves scrawled
with judgment, red flowers centered
with heavy-lidded eyes.

Vision

The one-eyed chicken
walks toward what it can see,
a circle ensnaring truth

A Journey of Many Days

Aphorisms for the Ear

The ear is the snail of the head.

An ear is a wax museum.

No one wants to drink in an ear garden.

He was up to his ears in ears.

An ear is the seashell of the head, echoing the ocean.

An ear is a cave that should not be explored.

If you were all ears, no one would talk to you.

The ears were ringing in the new year.

The sound circled the drain of the ear.

She smiled from ear to ear, a journey of many days.

A lobe is a path to love.

He gave a ring to her ear in promise.

The sow's ears were made of silk purses.

A heard of ears.

The ear curled into a ball and slept.

He followed the spiral of her ear and was lost.

Meditations on a Seashell

Lichen of the sand,
bowl of ocean,
with your sisters
the spirals, Sword
and Swirl, protective
luggage of soft, you
journey without ticket
or destination. Siamese
twins closed in a fist,
you open to feed.
Castanets in slow motion,
playing for no one, dance
forbidden. Outside the water,
you fade in sun, chip of
water's bone. When you are
broken into smallest pieces,
renamed sand,
you can no longer
hold the ocean.

Beach Trip

Sand is future glass, so get in the car,
fast-forward into Future, and stand
on the giant glass bridge of Beach.
We can listen to waves while we stare
at creatures frozen below, encapsulated–
there's a crab mid-stride and there's a plastic
cup. There will always be a band-aid, and we're lucky,
the washed-up jellyfish is under glass, just
step on it and laugh. Mostly there's just rock, though,
and it's too hard to sit on all day. Let's take the car
to the diner The Past. Let's stare at the window
and watch fish bones and shells, glistening in sun.

Capture

I'm going outside
to capture some
sky in this
bottle, take it
inside and pour
it down the drain
until the house
floats. A ship
around a bottle.

Burning the Ocean

The setting sun burns
down ocean and air, leaves
only black char we call *night*.
We breath in and become
our shadows, wait for
the chanting of daybreak to ring
out darkness. Fire rekindled from mirror.

Meditations on a Stone

Bones of air, you
hold nothing.
Weapon of first
and last resort,
drowner of kittens,
prison guard of
gems. If broken, you
multiply. First tool.
Beauty and boredom,
the cheekbones of the
earth. You make your
home in the pockets
of children. You live
in the throats
of birds, grinding
seed. You do not float,
but will dance on
water if asked right.
You are the home
of moss, the little
brother of mountains,
sand to giants.

Thunder

Sometimes night wakes up
in the middle of day.

The memory of warm breath on ear's spiral.
Like a voice whispering *thunder*,

and then thunder.
Electricity hovering like a kite

casting a shadow,
slice of night blown circling.

Outside the Window

The cloud bursts
open like over-ripened
fruit. The orange
left on counter
leaks from split skin. No
thoughts stick in my
mind this morning. Trapped
inside, the mind is a desert.

Dusk

And, just like that, the sun
is gone from the back side
of mountain, like the dead
suddenly rising and going out
for a walk in the field, perhaps
looking for a ripe dewberry or just
enjoying the sound of crickets
unwinding their spools,
like wool woven into a mat, a cover
to place over this cabin
as it lays down into earth.

Procession to the Morning

The shadows lie down, melting
into ground and air, settle in
to watch the show as the last
hares gather the scraps of day.
Star after star begins its trek
across sky echoed by
dream chasing nightmare
chasing dream. A coyote
climbs across the earth.
Frog songs meander
across the landscape, unsure
what direction to take. A single
bird flies across, unzipping
the eye as light spills.

After

After owls have eaten all your scattered thoughts,
    flying with heavy bellies;

After the sea has done nothing—marching back and forth blindly;

After the smoke has solidified to ash, and the stars
    have begun haunting your blood;

After night paws at your sleeping to get inside,
    sniffs the back of your throat;

The dawn cracks open, drains heavens—look how angels fall.

Meditations on Lichens

Half moons,
fingernails of a tree,
parentheses inside parentheses
inside parentheses, you are
the hidden meaning
unspoken in the woods,
what isn't heard
when a tree falls.
Alternating dark and light,
like a cloud-filled sky, you always
point north, to the star you love,
you are stairsteps to a
monument of fractals,
the small inside the large,
the stars of the forest, brittle
porcelain of nature,
plates serving air to air,
the erection of a tree
laying down, half buried
shield from a forgotten culture.

Monologue of a Possum's Shadow

You won't see me. My master sleeps
all day on top of me. But when we explore,
I hug the tree tighter than my master. When
she hisses, I laugh. When she gets scared,
she curls herself around me. I poke at her
to make her jump. We are best friends.
I only leave her side when she hangs
by her tail and I fly, or when she's
high in a tree and I stay on the ground
begging her to descend. We have babies.
Hers weigh her down but mine pull at me
to go up and up. They stretch me like dough
to the edge of the day.

Birches

Every day the birches
get their food of sky—
Heaven as manna from Heaven.
The birches nibble
day all day
until the sky is gone
then sleep—
soft birds kept
in cages of wood
like hearts nestled
among ribs.

Unmarred

You never come out of nature unmarred,
the blackberries tearing at your skin, begging
you to stay—crazed obsession. Or the ivy
that leaves you sleepless for days, the rock
that cut your foot to taste inside.
The bugs—nature's legs—burrowing, sapping, biting.
Even the garden, the tamed dog, scratches.
Cliff, river surge, tsunami, boulder, landslide.
Our ghosts call out from the forest, the ocean.
Hold your breath, don't answer.

A Moral History of Rivers

A river is a waterfall pretending to lie down in submission.
A river tramples rocks in their beds, erases their faces. A river
rushes past faceless rocks, pretending never to have met them.
A river has no history. You cannot fall into a river twice.
Egrets rush to a river in greeting, but when the river whispers
flood, they dissolve. A river gathers her children in her skirts to
watch them devour each other. A river steals from the mountain.
A river drains her basin. A river hides her gold in sunlight.
All rivers are nihilists rushing to their own oblivion. You cannot
kill a river, but you can increase her deadliness.

Monologue of a Horse's Shadow

I run on wind created by my master. On
open spaces, I stretch across grasses.
When my master sleeps, I run
through dreams, dark nightmare.

Asking for Tea

Aphorisms for a Mother

The nature of *mother* is nurture.

Motherhood necessitates invention.

Mamma knows breast.

The toddlers hunted the mother, an untidy expedition.

A mother might hover.

Yo mamma is so nice, she took care of you as a baby.
     Yo mamma looks very pretty today.

A mother is a country.

The angry mother was sourdough rising, clouding the room.

His mother tied him up in apron strings.

The mothers dug down into the earth, to return later.

The mothers poured down the mountain at dawn

A mother sat in his head, asking for tea.

A *Your Mother* Poem to the Moon

Moon, your mother is so dull she has to steal light from a lamp.

Moon, your mother is so poor the man on her is in rags,
    so poor she's never full.

Moon, your mother is made of processed cheese.

Moon, your mother hasn't ever been new.

Moon, your mother is so ugly only mangy dogs howl
    at her crater-face.

Moon, your mother is so stupid she orbits a TV satellite.

Moon, your mother's gravity is so weak it can't even
    cause a tide in a glass of water.

Moon, your mother is so lame she only inspired this stupid poem.

Gion Festival, Kyoto, 2018

Flooding delayed our trip by a week;
heat flooded our senses to
insensibility. July was finally here, with
its 1000-year parade to keep the plagues
from flooding in, with a float of the boy
emperor who enters the forest to select wood
for a temple, and a float holding the *chigo*, a boy
chosen as a messenger to the gods,
separated from his mother for the festival month.
He is a live child on a wooden float, although
others have wooden children.

There is a float
that tells of the ancestor of the emperors,
Amaterasu-Omikami, sun goddess who hid inside
a rock when she was angry, who made the sky
dark for days with her silence. This heat
is also the sun's wrath and people
pull a float with a moon in defiance.

When night finally comes, when Amaterasu-Omikami
sleeps, lanterns are lit to bring the moon to earth.
We slip, my children and I, behind the festival,
     deeper into the park,
deeper into night. A tanuki and her pups search
the trash for scraps. The mother turns her head
and stumbles off, heat-drunk in moonlight,
     leaving her babies behind.
We get so close we can almost touch them, these *chigos*.

We can almost let them whisper the words of the gods.

Creek

To hear water creaking
under ice-crusted rocks
is to hear the ghost of
spring. Frog croaks, cricket
chirps, bird rasps begging
for food. Shed your coats
to lighten the load. You can
hear banshees waking.

Venice, 1991/2016

Looking through time at the past
is like looking across a still lagoon
hazed through heat and humidity.
Truth is there, unclear.
                    At 19,
I stood near this Venetian water,
back to San Giorgio Maggiori, face
to St. Mark's Square. A pigeon
is perched on my head, trying to gain
footing but slipping and clawing, wings
stretched out for balance. We had woken
early to escape the heat. Light slipping
down the building to our heads and empty streets.
Delicious mornings, *we ripen standing still.*

Then I'm here again, adult and steady,
overlooking the narrow
Merceria, behind the golden horses,
through the back of the Clock Tower, through time,
and onto the square.
                  My daughter Olivia
is 12 and she stands still, face to St. Mark's Square,
arms outstretched, pigeons balanced perfectly
on her arms. She's a statue, the Lady of Pigeons,
the light on her hair is clarity. We
wander to the north end of the city,
where the streets empty of tour groups and heat,
step into the Church of Madonna dell'Orto, Tintoretto's,
to see the master's work, to share
what I know of beauty.

                              We see

The Miracle of St. Agnes and *Idolatry*
of the Golden Calf. A girl stares
out from *Presentation of the Virgin*
at Temple, drawing us into the crowded scene.
Olivia, love, is she you, or is she me?

Rise

As if the greenhouse tent
could rise into sky,
the dove rose against it,
strange would-be turtledove.
After the sun went down
below earth, I came out
of my shelter and heard
beating of wings against night.
I lifted the white frame
from soft earth, spread
open like a wing, loosed
another spirit into air.

The Owl Feather

When he picked up the feather
from the forest, when
he realized it held
the heartbeat of the owl,
when he saw how it moved
with the small wind, or
the tremble from hand,
when he realized the feather was
the living part of the hollow
structure we call *owl*,
he freed it a second time.

The Waiting Room

Let's take a look into the room
where the dead wait to be born again—
the absolute boredom of it.
It is a room inside the castle of string theory,
where no nouns exist, only verbs:
looking, hovering, being (but only sort of).
The room is a tree, shimmering a little in light breeze.
A tree which, at dusk, turns into a flock of green parakeets lifting.

Ghosts and Mirrors

Ghosts appear in candlelit mirrors. You can
create a spirit road by facing mirrors. Ghosts
might get lost, or trapped on the wrong side like
turtles helped out of traffic. Bloody Mary
is a ghost you have to summon. You are
Mary's Uber. Narcissus was trapped by
a mirror until he became a ghost. A
mirror reflecting sleep can make you sick. Mirrors
lowered into a well predict if you
recover or become like Narcissus.
Breaking a mirror is seven years' bad luck;
you can't become a ghost for seven years.
To keep ghosts out, cover mirrors. But they're still
there, napping parakeets, waiting for you.

Abisko, Sweden, 2016

We take the train overnight, sleeping in stacks
three high like firewood, our bodies
ghosted by motion. Refusing to believe
the earth could be still, we hike into night,
through woods stunted from huddling
through months of night.

It's summer, and the calendar
ticking off days is as meaningless as a clock counting seconds.

The water in the sky reflects onto the water on the ground.
We can't find our grounding. We find the white ghost
wing of a ptarmigan, caught by fox and winter.

A wolverine will take a reindeer,
and another, and another, for the love
of the kill, like ice chewing through rock. We can hear
ice crunch like bone beneath our feet, beneath ground.
We soak our feet in a pool and fish chew
our skin. Annika catches one, because sometimes
destruction is like that, sometimes it can be caught,
a wolverine skin in a yurt.

I have a picture of you, Annika,
standing on a mountain in the Arctic, you are the top
of the top of the world, sky around your shoulders
like a pelt.

Willow Ptarmigan

If the Willow Ptarmigan was taken down
by the arctic fox, on the rocks
on the frozen hill, then the stones
are left dreaming of wings. If the stones
gain feathers and flight, if they leave their
density to the snow, the stars have reason
to tremble, they are lost. If the stars are lost,
they must look to the village for direction,
the herder huts, the winter settlements
of nomads. If the directions
are imprecise, then shadows wander,
even the air holds its breath.

Rock Ptarmigan Wing, Winter Morph

A white wing on the mountain—solid,
solo, no brother—as if the fox only needed
one toy after his meal.
This is one way to know we have stumbled
in Arctic; another, the lack
of anything taller than ice-worn rock.
Blank space all the way to sun. If you pick up
this relic, this beacon, it might
crumble in your hand like a dream
of flight at sunrise. *Lagopus* (hare foot) *muta*
(silence personified), white in winter,
brown in summer. Brothers
visiting all that is left of angel.

The Birds of Costa Rica, 2014

The night before our drive, a monkey had given birth, and her family
screamed their excitement up to the heavens, and down into our heads.
They continued throughout morning, outshouting the Great Kiskadee
and Shining Honeycreeper, past Manakin and Forest-Falcon.

From the coast, from the Yellow-Throated Toucan and Yellow-Crowned
Night Heron, we drove hours into the air of Costa Rica,
     across the American
isthmus to the Cerro de la Muerte, so far in the clouds it brought us to
our knees. The chef brought herb tea to settle us, a welcome
       to this Heaven.

We were on a quest for the Resplendent Quetzal, emerald with
red tail drawing eye to sky, with black thoughtless eyes brimming
night. We were tired, although our coastal hotel had been comfortable,
a place for us and our young, and the howler monkeys and theirs.

Now in the mountains, we could sip tea and watch the blue of the Black-
Faced Solitaire sipping herbs outside our door, the hummingbirds
     (the Lancebill,
the Violetear, the Woodstar, the Mountain-Gems) gathering around
       vines
at the trout farm, Long-Tailed Silky Flycatchers flagging feathers
       over cloud forest.

Morning after morning we would wake at daybreak to follow a guide
       to the
edge, calling the Quetzal, hearing his reply, his body staying hidden
       behind trees.
He sent his call to sniff us, and found us wanting. On our last day, we
newly-acclimated residents of clouds, welcomed by the howling
       of Acorn

Woodpeckers, set out again before breakfast. On a limb held up by
   the air itself
was a new-birthed Quetzal, resting after his meal. His colors were dull,
but his eyes were dark and bottomless. The eyes of a dream
just out of its shell, night laid out at its feet.

Meditations on Grass

You gather in
multitudes, wearers
of frost, swords
held up in a charge
frozen in time.
In warmer air, you
cushion picnickers
while holding armies
of biting insects.
Soft hair of soil,
precursor to weave
and nest, almsgiver
to the small, whether
furry or shelled or
feathered. You hide
young from all but the reaper.
Green whistle calling to wind,
you wave to the clouds,
who never give you
a ride. You gather to hear
the speech of the trees, gather
the speech of the trees to bury.

A Brief History of a Song

It started with a rumble under
rocks, ice melting with crackles,
burbles and then a ptarmigan
drank it, drummed
its throat until a fox ate
the ptarmigan and the song
stuck fast, became garbled,
weird and the fox coughed it
up, so it returned to the ground
on the feet of a beetle, who died,
migrated into melted earth until
the song built up energy, pressure,
was thrown from the lungs of earth,
rained down, hardened in ocean,
which had rhythm and talent and went far,
taught the dolphins who taught the gulls,
who never got it right but sang loudly and eventually
a songbird picked up the scraps and, being
crafty, made something better of it.

To Annika and Olivia,
On the Occasion of Their Birthday

Once I was a vessel carrying you:

    seeds in a hull,

        treasure of a new land,

            moths crept deep into fur before bursting out

                    in a rainstorm as

    stars.

Once you were infants.

    Now you stand:

        trees to break storm in a field,

            holding a nest of all my shining hopelings.

The Very Lip
of Her
Lip

Aphorisms for Lips

One lip is the reflection of the other.

Two lips are a rose.

Lips attack in pairs. He should never have approached them.

Lips are tongue-tamers.

Lips try to learn from the teeth how to bite.

Lips spread like honey across her face.

He studied her lips but forgot how to read.

Two lips eloped.

Lips ran to the ears with the news.

Two feral lips peeked out from the beard.

A lip is a trap for pray.

He went to the very lip of her lip and fell in.

Lips cushioned his fall.

Valentine Poem

Darkness lays down
across the room
like a dog, curling.

The dimming sounds of
the house circle
the air with the fan.

Sleep creeps in
to steal the feeling
of lying next to you.

A Poem Consisting of Stolen Lines

From what huge darkness was this heavy night chipped,

tired as a hand after the war.

We'd lay our heads down on the heavy side,

    the one that doesn't give out dreams.

The dank earth dreams, everything around you spills over,

time flowed like blood from a child's slit throat.

A different comfort suits us now, a different discomfort.

A fire morosely chewed the darkness,

the ashes of the stars.

Now we know that even the air is matter that weighs us down.

The air is one soft wing.

Memory sometimes has no memory of itself.

Trust the darkness when the light lies.

I will bring his bones back to you.

Cleaning Day

I dusted the shadows from
the corners, knocked
them to the carpet,
vacuumed them up, emptied
the canister into the thick,
black trash bag, tied
it, but couldn't lift it
to the curb. Oh,
the heavy shadows of the heart!

Meditations on Flame

Light as object, shapeless
shape, necessary
danger, you eat
your home. You are
pure dance tethered
by a tail, dancer who cannot
be held, snapping
with no fingers,
raising your hands
to sun, desperate to
leave earth, throwing
auguries into air,
stealing color, leaving ash.

Gothic

Light limps across the graveyard waiting to die
    and sink into the nearest plot.

The sound of a key in a padlock roosts in a tree and settles
    for the night.

Your hand brushes a stone wall and a gathering of moths
    explodes into stars.

Then you speak to me in a language long lost to the distant future.

Monologue of a Cow's Shadow

I raise my mouth to drink the sky,
while my master eats the earth.
We kiss sometimes. I am a plow.
My legs reach up and my
horns push into the ground.
Milk flows from me when my sky-baby
suckles, or the calloused hands of
sky-man tug. I run on fog. In the
hot afternoons, I stretch, to see
how far I can wander from my master.
At dusk, I break free.

A
Horrible
Thing

Aphorisms for the Hand

A hand is a better stone than a cup.

A hand is the dead-end of the arm.

The palm is the soil to the fingers.

To literally give someone a hand is a horrible thing.

A hand is the armadillo of the body.

What has four fingers and a thumb? This hand!

A hand is a wave removed from time.

She said to the bird, "What is a hand in the bush worth?"

The palm tells the future but the back of the hand keeps
    a poker face.

Fingers are so close to being free.

A hand will only count to five in warning.

A hand can be a ball or a paddle.

A hand curls around nothingness, holds it close.

Cat Love

The cat loves his kill,
walks around it in
circles, nuzzles it
softly, purrs
into its wounds,
wants to bring it inside
his soft belly.

Paw

Sometimes when asleep
I feel the cat's paw
press gently on neck,
      warm, furred.
Slowly claws extract,
wrap the beat of blood,
contemplate desire.

Stray

We saw him only one
morning, hound-chased
and hissing from the fence
he only just managed
to stumble up before falling
to safety on the other side.
Out of his territory he was
just another ancient exiled king
hiding from the gods.

Hatching

We came home to a bedroom
humming of a dozen newly-hatched wasps.

Outside Spring was stretching, raising
its arms into air.

We slammed the door, searched
the internet for remedies, frantic.

Spring was unstoppable, gorgeous with
yellow pollen, temperatures already 80.

Each wasp was sucked into the vacuum's accordion tube,
wings pulled backwards, the moment of struggle was over.

Then the air filled with absence.

The songs of birds everywhere. You can't walk
a dozen feet without running into one, cobwebs of sound.

Inside the vacuum the wasps crawl,
dust covered, slowing dust to dust.

Damp earth sprouts every kind of blooming weed and
each day, a dozen more from the vent, Gaia birthing winged Titans.

Imagine the Rats

Imagine the rats as wildlife and our sightings
become a gift. The fox at the edge
of the field. An otter surfacing to dark.
Take the soft gray of rat fur, the smallness
of paws, the comings from the nest
under the shed, across the yard, feet
from your chair, make you hold
your breath.

Mouse

The mouse
collects footfalls
to make a nest,
gives birth
to a litter of winds.

Seed

Everything starts with a seed; this poem, for example. I watered
and watched them every day at first—not able to tell the carrots
from the weeds until the second leaves unfold.

When we got it from the dog's mouth, it was small, eyes closed,
unmoving on the floor but not dead, not yet. The dog was gentle
with the creature she dug out from under the dresser. What was it,
this outsider? Was it mouse, or squirrel, or rat?

The second leaves are frilled and bright green, small, delicate.
You must thin them, give them room, kill some to save the others.
You try to pick the strongest of the wisps, and trim the others with
scissors, one by one.

Visitors is what the Bible calls angels. In Sodom they were
vulnerable. Their host offers his children to the crowd, to do with
what they please. Kill some to save the others.

Soon after we pry the dog's mouth, after we gently place the infant
in a bag, after we crush the skull with our heel, weeks later,
we see a mother squirrel carrying a folded baby over half her size
in her mouth. The child clings to her. We watch this mother
teaching this one that's left to gather leaves from broccoli, fold
them, bunch them into cheeks to carry to safety.

It's becoming colder at night. We shut our children's windows
to keep out the cold, to protect. Only some of us are made to see
the Spring.

What the aerialist thought
while falling 1.6 seconds to her death

To travel this world is a river, love; to cross

paths is wonder. There are no photos

of what hasn't been done.

Only a tornado pulls objects up—only destruction

leaves this earth.

I have taken a great leap;

I have gone into the vast silence; I am carried

away by the stream of birth and death. I am

defenseless.

If you can list all magic books,

is that itself a spell? Life goes on

only if you're a small target, a hare not jumping

in the open.

Compassionate ones, forget not

your ancient vows.

Silk burns the skin if taken too fast.

A falling body unzips sky. I have become the voice

that breaks the earth, that causes the crack that lets the seed in.

What the aerialist's boyfriend thought as she fell to her death

The night collapses slowly on itself like a rotting house.
Water could never hold its shape against gravity—
but she was fire.
            The air shatters as she falls through it—
shards in my lungs. I want her
to be a tornado—to pull up from ground. But she
is a flock of birds nesting. She is ash, precipitate of sky.

Wake

Unfold these words
in a dark hollowness of an ancient church.
Light a candle for the dead; read
them. Then light a candle for the living
to set the Book of the Dead on fire.
Send the night staggering down
the empty street like a drunk.
Blow out the candles, stamp
the flames—there is nothing left.

The moon is disappearing into the fields

The moon is disappearing into the fields as
war approaches the horizon. Morning crawls
from a crack and seeks a cave to hide. The crows
refuse to cede the morning to the doves.
Our shadows cling to us for warmth. How do we unfold
the shrouds that holds our souls? How
do we lift them from sleep like angels in the Last Judgement?
How do we not let the path walk off itself and be lost?
There are holes all over the earth that lead the way
to the underworld. There are fewer mountains for the gods to live.
It seems we already know we will sink into the ground
like our whispers. Despite sky burials and cliff coffins,
we mostly still place our dead in the earth,
and expect them to stay.

This is a poem to say I'm sorry

One dog had just died, so when the second
beautiful, long-eared, stubborn hound's
gait slowed we assumed she had
the same stone of grief inside her as we did.

When she bit you, trying to lift her,
we rushed her to the car, carefully driving.
We listened to the vet, who said
she only pulled a muscle.

When she refused to climb the stairs
to our room, you and I took turns sleeping
on the downstairs floor by her side.
Our heads were full of lies and selfishness.

We thought we could fix her with love,
with spoonfuls of food coaxed into mouth.
She loved us, so she ate them, and lived a while longer.
Forgive me, loyal ghost.

Love Poem

The cat was near death
when we found him
in the tub, wet in vomit.
Although we weren't sure
if we liked the cat,
and we were sure
he didn't like us, we paid
a month's salary to save him.
We kept the dog
to the point, in retrospect,
of cruelty. We rescued
the chicken from a hawk, poured
disinfectant over bone,
removed an eye,
and kept her in the house,
unnatural pet.
It's unclear if we love animals,
or only hate death.
I love you. What will I do to you
when you are weak?

Rat

So many animals we fought
to keep alive, but the rat
we could not kill.
He moved into the bathroom
so we set the trap, stuffed
towels underneath the door
and waited. He stayed
next to the clawed foot
of the tub, hidden from light
for three days until finally,
he ate the poison, soaked
in honey, mellification of a saint.

St Sebastian in the Afterlife

Eternity for me is sand
through a sieve. I was shot
full of arrows for my first
martyrdom. I was rescued,
only to be clubbed to death
for my second. A misshapen
sieve is my fate. Prayers
sift through me, scattered across
Heaven. Only the heavy ones
get caught in the mesh of me.
I am slowly sinking from their weight.

St Barnabas in the Afterlife

Heaven is just a storage locker for ghosts with no one to haunt.
I spend my days wringing out the laundry of my flesh, airing it
like a braid of garlic from the ceiling. My martyrdom
requires upkeep—patching and darning, and always
the slipping of the parts of me that haven't yet let go.

Monologue of a Fly's Shadow

My master flies and alights, flies
and alights, and I am a yoyo
constantly dragged to next.
When my master lands on a meal,
fleshy half-spoiled fruit or rotting
meat of death, I am solidly in it,
covered in muck. It's no wonder
I'm stuck to the ground, unable
to fly. When the rains come,
I disappear with the light, unable
to get clean. One day, a hand will
land and my master will become covered in me.

The Reason Ötzi Died

Ötzi was hiking alone, with a fat wallet. The path was isolated,
    and he was the easiest mark. He was easy for you.

Ötzi had stolen your wallet, and you chased him into the wood
    for revenge.

Ötzi had stolen your wallet and, after a fair trial,
    was taken to the mountains for justice.

Ötzi was the chief's first son. You were the chief's second son.
    You followed him into the wood.

Ötzi had wanted a girl (was it you?) that wasn't his.
    He had taken her. He was chased to the mountains for justice.
    The girl's body decomposed over a thousand years.

Ötzi had wanted you. You weren't his but you loved him.
    Your father chased him into the wood for revenge.

Ötzi was the pure sacrifice to the gods to end the sickness
    spreading through your body.

Ötzi rejected the gods and taught a new religion. You threw the
    gods to the ground, shaved your head, fasted. He left his body
    to save your world.

St Peter in the Afterlife

I was a fisherman, a laborer, the first Pope,
a rock, the founder of churches, settler of squabbles,
tireless traveler, but I don't even have a retirement.
I'm the damned doorman of Heaven.
I barely sit before another knock at the door, another
request to check the book "one more time" before
sending a soul down the street to the next gate.
The key itself weighs more than all the useless,
lazy angels. If only there was another rest after this,
if only another death.

Night as a Dog

A dog steps backwards, behind
itself and disappears. A black
dog becomes the night. The night
is what it eats, a black dog. Night
growls in the shadows.
Night whines for scraps
of lamplight. Night fetches whatever
thoughts were flung into the winds of day.
Night paws your hand, gently taking it
into mouth. The night is what it eats.
Loyal night, lay down and dream
a furry body around our hearts.

Childhood

My childhood is memories of a thicket in Ellijay,
a tilted mountain where rough walnuts tumbled.
There were lady's slippers flung off from the cardinals.
We became goats running the slope.

But really there was a trash truck always parked
on the side of the street, and puddles in the dirt lot,
and a house with pieces falling off and down the hillside,
a house stepping off into clouds.

Picking Basil at Night

A pinch at the base of leaf
then into the bowl, leaving
fragrance to stand guard
like Athena. Heat is taking
flight and night air settles,
a bird in a nest. When the
bowl is full, one goes inside
where light is making
its last stand against dark;
air is pine nuts roasting.
Golden oil streams
like a goddess's hair in the light
pulses of blender. We tell
stories for centuries because
they feed us, fill the senses.
The pesto fills jars and nestles
into the cold light of fridge.
Basil-scented hands hold victory, dream.

Weeds

But all of these long
sun-punished days
the weeds believed
you carried jars
of cool water
for them

Poem Dedications and Notes

"Hawk" is dedicated to Verania White

"Aphorisms for the Eyes" is dedicated to Julia Beach

"St Denis in the Afterlife" is for Magnus Egerstedt

"Meditations on Lichens" is for Wendy Truran

"Monologue of a Possum's Shadow" is dedicated to Annie Peterle, the Possum Queen

"A Moral History of Rivers" is dedicated to Trudy Nan Boyce

"Aphorisms for a Mother" is for Jean Hanson

"Ghosts and Mirrors" is dedicated to Katie Farris

"A Brief History of Song" is for Karen Hood Hopkins

"What the aerialist thought while falling 1.6 seconds to her death" and *"What the aerialist's boyfriend thoughts as she fell to her death"* are dedicated to my daughters' first aerial teacher, Jacosa Kato. The italics in this poem are from the Buddhist memorial prayer.

The Aphorism poems are patterned after work by Ramón Gómez de la Serna.
The Monologue of a Shadow poems are inspired by *"Monologue of a Vulture's Shadow"* by Eduardo C. Corral. The Saint poems are inspired by the saint stories and sacred art. Their stories are wild. *"Childhood"* is patterned after a poem by Antonio Machado.

The italicized line in *"Venice 1991/2016"* comes from *"The women ripen standing still"* in Cesare Pavese's *"Grappa in September"* (trans. William Arrowsmith).

The lines of *"A Poem Consisting of Stolen Lines 2"* are stolen from, in order, Attila Jozsef (trans. John Batki), Vladimir Holan (trans. C.G. Hanzlicek and Dana Habova), Odysseas Elytis (trans. Edmund Keeley and Philip Sherrard), Eugenio Montale (trans. William Arrowsmith), Nazim Hikmet (trans. Randy Blasing and Mutlu Konuk), and Henry Morton Stanley.

Ötzi, also known as Iceman, and is a natural mummy discovered in the Alps. His cause of death is unknown, and much researched.

Thank you to Susannah Appelbaum and Codhill Press for rescuing this stranded project and for being a welcome literary home. I am so honored to be a part of the Codhill family. Thank you to Dana Curtiss and Elixir Press for her belief and time with this work. Thank you to Ilya Kaminsky, Rigoberto Gonzalez, and Jenny Sadre-Orafai for their time and kind words. Thanks to Richard Jackson, Tito (Alberto Rios), Norman Dubie, and Beckian Fritz Goldberg for their mentoring. I thank you to my fellow classmates and workshop friends at UIC and ASU for helping develop my voice. Thank you to my Atlanta workshop, especially Katie Farris, Elly Bookman, and Emily Heilker. I hope my voice occasionally speaks during your editing as yours does in mine. Many of these poems were developed at the Hambidge Center and during the Tupelo Press 30/30 Project. This manuscript has been on the short or long list at several presses, and this has helped me not give up on it, so thank you for the readers and editors at the Vassar Miller Prize, 42 Miles Press, Word Works, White Pine Press, Idaho Prize, and Marsh Hawk Press. Thank you to the Grant Park Coven and the Southeast Atlanta Lady MOB for their friendship and support. And, always, to my family: Magnus, Annika, Olivia, and my parents Jean and Dan, and nieces Susan and Kellina.

Acknowledgements

Apricity Magazine: *The Waiting Room, The moon is disappearing into the fields* (2020)

ArLiJo: *The Owl Feather* (2019)

Burningword Literary Journal: *Beach Trip* (2019)

Common Ground Review: *Abisko, Sweden, 2016* (2024)

The Comstock Review: *What the aerialist thought while falling 1.6 seconds to her death, What the aerialist's boyfriend thought as she fell to her death* (2017)

Illuminations Magazine: *A Your Mother Poem to the Moon* (2023)

{isacoustic}: *Cat Love, Mouse* (2018), *Meditations on Lichens, Meditations on Flame, Meditation on Grass* (2020)

The Maynard: *Monologue of a Cow's Shadow, Monologue of a Fly's Shadow* (2020), *Naming* (2018)

Paper Dragon: *Meditations on a Stone* (2022)

Plume: *A Writer's Companion: Meditations on a Stone, Aphorisms for a Hand, A Moral History of Rivers, Venice 1991/2016, Gion Festival Kyoto 2018, The Birds of Costa Rica, The Invention of the Feather Bed, Weeds, St Peter in the Afterlife, St Agnes in the Afterlife* (2020)

Poetry Miscellany: *Saint Barnabas in the Afterlife, Night as a Dog* (2022)

Red River Review: *Willow Ptarmigan* (2017)

riverSedge: *Birches* (2020), *Unmarred* (2021)

Stirring: *Childhood* (2019), *Aphorisms for the Hair* (2021)

Virga: *Capture* (2020)

Beach Trip was nominated for a Best of the Net Award in 2020.

Ghosts and Mirrors was featured on the October 2023 episode of the podcast Plume: A Writer's Companion.

About The Author

Danielle Hanson is author of *Fraying Edge of Sky* (Codhill Press Poetry Prize) and *Ambushing Water* (Finalist, Georgia Author of the Year Awards), and editor of *Objects in This Mirror* (Press 53, co-edited with Julia Beach) and *Sightlines: View Points on Susheel Kumar Sharma's The Door is Half Open* (Paragon International). Her poetry was the basis for a puppet show at the Center for Puppetry Arts. She is Marketing Director for Sundress Publications, and serves on their Editorial Board. She curated a poet/artist collaboration show *Alloy* at Arts Beacon in Atlanta, where she was Poet-in-Residence. Previously, she has also been Writer-in-Residence for Georgia Writers, Poetry Editor for Hayden's Ferry Review, and Poetry Editor for Doubleback Books. Her work has appeared in over 100 journals. She is Writer in Residence at the University of California, Irvine and serves as the inaugural Poet Laureate of Costa Mesa, California.